MY MOM IS AN ONLINE SELLER

By
Ann Compio
Mirjana Ivanka Compio
Bimby Macbs Compio

By Ann Compio, Mirjana Ivanka Compio, Bimby Macbs Compio

ISBN:
Hardbound-978-621-470-769-0
Softbound/Paperback-978-621-470-770-6
PDF (downloadable)-978-621-470-771-3

Published by:
Poetry Planet Book Publishing House
Rosario, Pozorrubio, Pangasinan, Philippines
Contact Number: 09554960094
Email: maritesritumalta@gmail.com

DEDICATION

Together with my daughter Mirjana and our precious Avery, I respectfully dedicate this book to God Almighty, who is the fountainhead of all goodness and love in the universe. We are profoundly appreciative of His heavenly protection and bountiful help all along the way.

Thank you, Mama and Papa, for instilling in me the importance of sticking to goals and working hard no matter what obstacles may arise. Although you are no longer physically there in my life, I will always carry your love and wisdom with me.

Thank you for always believing in me and pushing me to reach for the stars, my darling siblings, whose unfailing love and encouragement have been a constant source of strength.

Thank you, Jerome, for being my steadfast rock and consistent pillar of support in my online selling ventures. Your undying faith in me has given me the fortitude to constantly pursue my goals. Your unwavering support means the world to me.

Finally, I want to express my deep appreciation to all of my business partners (suppliers and customers) whose confidence and support have been crucial to my success. Your support and collaboration have been crucial to my development.

This book is dedicated to the belief that faith, love, and perseverance can change the world. With God's help, I pray that this encourages and emboldens everybody who reads it to go after their goals with unyielding zeal.

With affection and appreciation,

Ann

PREFACE

In today's highly connected world, we hear inspiring accounts of those who have found their way to success in the online world. One journey, in particular, stands out among others; it's a story of motherly love, shared aspirations, and essential life lessons. You've found the home of "My Mom Is an Online Seller."

This book celebrates a mother and daughter's special relationship by following them as they launch an online business. As the world moves toward a more digital future, our protagonist learns not only the art of business, but also the value of patience, trust, and originality. This moving story is meant to encourage and motivate young people to develop their entrepreneurial spirit so that they can meet the challenges of a changing world.

Readers follow this mother-daughter duo as they share their stories of self-discovery, family dynamics, and lessons learned while building a thriving online business. This book is more than just a collection of heartwarming anecdotes and life lessons; it's also a guide that can help readers maintain and improve a system that provides them happiness and thankfulness as they accept the gift of internet sales.

From creating an online presence to growing a dedicated clientele, the reader will see the transformational power of the entrepreneurial spirit as the story unfolds. The mother's words of advice are reflective of the years of hard work, conquering challenges, and appreciating each opportunity to interact with consumers and make a difference that she has accumulated.

In "My Mom is an Online Seller," we hope to convey the essence of a unique mother-daughter bond while also honoring the support that loved ones may offer along the path to entrepreneurship. This book serves as a gentle reminder that business success is measured not just by material gains but also by the quality of the connections and principles that are fostered along the road.

I hope that people of all ages will be encouraged by this narrative to pursue their aspirations, make use of the many possibilities the Internet offers, and learn valuable lessons from the unlikeliest of places. Follow along as we explore the inspiring and instructive tale of "My Mom is an Online Seller."

TABLE OF CONTENTS

My Mom Is
an Online
Seller

Mirjana was playing with her little sister Avery and cousin Mutya when she noticed her mother, Ann, was always on her phone. She asked her mother what she was doing, and Ann replied that she was selling things online. Mirjana was curious and asked how she did it. Ann explained that she had her own online store and sold things like clothes and accessories. Mirjana was amazed and asked if she could help her mother sell things too. This was the beginning of Mirjana's journey into the world of online selling.

Ann showed Mirjana how to take pictures of the items she was selling and how to write descriptions for them. Mirjana was excited to help and took pictures of a few items. The next day, Ann received a notification that one of the items had been sold. Mirjana was thrilled and couldn't wait to help her mother sell more things. This first sale gave Mirjana a taste of the excitement and satisfaction that comes with online selling.

Ann explained to Mirjana that it was important to provide good customer service to keep customers coming back. She showed Mirjana how to package the items and write a thank you note to the customer. Mirjana was happy to help and wrote a nice note to the customer who had purchased the item. This experience taught Mirjana the value of treating customers well and the impact it can have on a business.

Ann told Mirjana that social media was a great way to promote her online store. She showed her how to take pictures of the items and post them on social media. Mirjana was excited to help and posted pictures of the items on her own social media accounts. Soon, her friends and family were asking about the items and some even made purchases. This chapter highlights the power of social media in reaching a wider audience and generating more sales.

Ann explained to Mirjana that it was important to be honest about the items she was selling. She told her that if there were any defects or issues with the items, she needed to disclose them to the customer. Mirjana understood and made sure to check the items carefully before posting them online. This chapter emphasizes the importance of honesty and transparency in online selling, which builds trust with customers and leads to repeat business.

After a few weeks of helping her mother, Mirjana was excited to see that they had made a good amount of money from the online store. Ann showed her how to keep track of the sales and expenses. Mirjana was happy to see that her hard work had paid off and that they could use the money for something special. This chapter explores the satisfaction and rewards that come with online selling, including the ability to earn money and achieve financial goals.

As Mirjana continued to help her mother with the online store, she realized that it was important to manage her time well. She made sure to finish her homework and chores before helping her mother. Ann was proud of Mirjana for being responsible and managing her time well. This chapter highlights the importance of time management skills in online selling, which requires balancing multiple responsibilities and priorities.

“Mirjana
Interviewed
Her Mom
Ann"

Mirjana was struggling to come up with an idea for her journalism assignment. She needed to interview someone about how they balance their work and personal life. Suddenly, she had an idea. She turned to her mom, who was working on her laptop, and asked if she could interview her about how she manages to juggle being an online seller, a mom, and a wife. Her mom agreed, and Mirjana was excited to get started on her project.

Ann was happy to help her daughter with her journalism assignment. She asked Mirjana how she could assist her with the project. Mirjana was grateful for her mom's willingness to help and asked her first question. She wanted to know what sparked her mom's initial curiosity about becoming an internet retailer. Ann thought for a moment before answering and began to share her story with her daughter.

Ann leaned back in her chair and began to tell her daughter about how she and her husband were looking for ways to supplement their income. They decided to sell some of their unused possessions through an online auction and saw how simple it was to make a transaction. This sparked their interest in expanding their sales efforts. Ann continued to explain how they turned their small sales into a full-fledged business.

Mirjana was fascinated by her mom's story and asked how they turned their small sales into a thriving business. Ann explained that it took a lot of hard work and dedication. They started by selling items they no longer needed or used and then began buying items in bulk to resell online. Before they knew it, they had a successful business. Mirjana was impressed by her mom's entrepreneurial spirit.

Mirjana was curious about how her mom managed to juggle her work and family responsibilities. Ann admitted that it wasn't always easy, but she tried to set boundaries and prioritize her time. She made sure to spend quality time with her children and husband while also making time for her business. Mirjana was impressed by her mom's ability to balance everything and asked how she did it.

Ann smiled and explained that having her husband's support was crucial to her success. He helped with the business when he could and was always there to lend a listening ear or a helping hand. Mirjana realized that having a strong support system was important for achieving her goals. She thanked her mom for sharing her story and inspiring her to pursue her dreams.

Mirjana closed her notebook and looked up at her mom. She thanked her for sharing her story and inspiring her to pursue her dreams. Ann reminded her daughter that anything was possible if she worked hard and followed her passions. Mirjana felt empowered and excited to share her mom's story with her class. She realized that she too could achieve her goals with hard work and determination.

Mirjana walked away from the interview feeling inspired and motivated. She realized that her mom's story was a testament to the power of hard work and perseverance. She couldn't wait to share her mom's story with her class and inspire others to pursue their passions. Mirjana felt grateful for her mom's support and knew that she could achieve anything she set her mind to.

Mirjana was grateful for the opportunity to help her mother with the online store. She realized that online selling was a great way to make money and that it was something she could do in the future. Ann was happy to see that Mirjana had learned so much and was excited about the possibilities for the future. This final chapter reflects on the lessons learned and the potential for online selling as a viable career path or side hustle.

Helping
Her Mom
In Selling

Mirjana and her little sister Avery were playing in the living room when they heard their mom, Ann, crying in the kitchen. They rushed to see what was wrong and found her looking at a cake with a slight damage. She explained that a customer refused to take it because of the damage caused by the delivery rider. Ann had put a lot of effort into baking and decorating the cake, and it was disheartening to see it go to waste. Mirjana and Avery felt sad seeing their mom in tears and wanted to do something to help her feel better.

Mirjana felt bad seeing her mom so sad. She thought of a way to help her mom. She told her mom not to worry because she and Avery had some savings. They could use it to buy the cake and pray to God for more customers. Ann was surprised by her daughter's thoughtfulness and agreed to her plan. Mirjana's idea gave Ann hope and made her feel grateful for her kind and generous daughters. She felt blessed to have such caring children who were willing to help her in her time of need.

The next day, Mirjana and Avery went to their mom's online store and bought the cake. They also added some frozen products to their cart. After the purchase, they prayed to God to bless their mom's business and give her more customers. Mirjana and Avery felt happy and proud of themselves for being able to help their mom. They knew that their little act of kindness and prayer could make a big difference in their mom's life. They were excited to see what God had in store for their family's business.

The next few days were busy for Ann's online store. She received more orders from different customers. Mirjana and Avery were happy to see their mom smiling again and busy with her business. They knew that their little act of kindness and prayer made a big difference. They felt proud of their mom's hard work and dedication, and they were grateful for the new customers who were supporting their family's business. They felt blessed to be part of such a loving and supportive family.

At dinner, the family talked about how God answered their prayers and blessed their mom's business. They thanked Mirjana and Avery for their idea and generosity. They also reminded each other to always trust in God's timing and to be patient in difficult situations. The family felt grateful for each other and for the love and support they shared. They felt blessed to have each other and to be able to rely on God's guidance and grace. After dinner, Mirjana suggested a new plan to help her mom's business. She thought of making a video of their family baking and decorating cakes together. They could post it on their mom's online store and social media accounts to attract more customers.

Ann and Avery loved the idea and they started planning for it. Mirjana felt excited to be able to contribute to her mom's business in a creative way. She felt proud of her family's teamwork and dedication to making their business successful.

With the help of Mirjana's new plan and God's blessings, Ann's online store became more successful than ever. They received more orders and positive feedback from satisfied customers. Mirjana and Avery were proud of their mom and happy to be part of her business. They learned that even small acts of kindness and prayers can make a big impact. They felt grateful for their family's love and support, and they felt blessed to be able to share their talents and creativity with others. They knew that with God's guidance, their family could overcome any obstacle and achieve great things.

ONLINE SELLER POETRY

"PAY YOUR ORDER"

PAY YOUR ORDER

Selling online is a joyous sight
Yet customers can give us a fright
They order with a click so sly
And act like they'll pay, no need to try
But when the bill arrives, they flee
Far away from responsibility

Promises of payment, oh so soon
Weeks turn to months, like a bad cartoon
Reminders and emails we send with care
But met with cold and stubborn air

Suffering revenue, waning patience
Our troubles seem to never cease
We strive to find a way to thrive
But obstacles block our path with ease
We yank at our locks,
In efforts to keep our minds
From slipping away
Steadfast and true, we sell with glee
Online commerce, our destiny

Through thick and thin, we persevere
Our passion for selling is crystal clear
Oh, customers who don't pay on time
Your tardiness is quite a crime
We kindly ask for prompt payment
To avoid any further engagement
Please settle your dues without delay

And keep our business in a steady way

Your credit, dear friend, Soon to be but a dime
Remember this, I implore, In these trying times.
New buyers we'll seek, who'll pay without delay,
And soon enough, you'll be left in disarray.
Pay your bills, don't be a jerk,
Or your business will go berserk.
Online selling is a game of fun,
But with serious aims, it must be done

"HAPPY CUSTOMER"

HAPPY CUSTOMER

A visitor came to our digital store
In search of something they yearned for
With eagerness and optimism in their soul
They clicked and browsed through every scroll.

Behold, they found their treasure
A prize beyond all measure.
With a smile so bright, they took out their measure, Their happiness, and contentment, more and more

As they made the purchase, without any doubt
Their confidence and courage shone throughout.
With a speedy pace, we shipped it out
Ensuring they'd receive it, no doubt.

At their door, the package did arrive
Excitement they couldn't help but contrive.
A voice filled with gratitude and glee
Left a review, so quietly

Praising our worth and service so fine
Making their shopping a joy divine.

Our happy customer, we thank thee, For trusting us with thy purchase and glee, We promise to go the extra mile, And make thy shopping experience worthwhile.

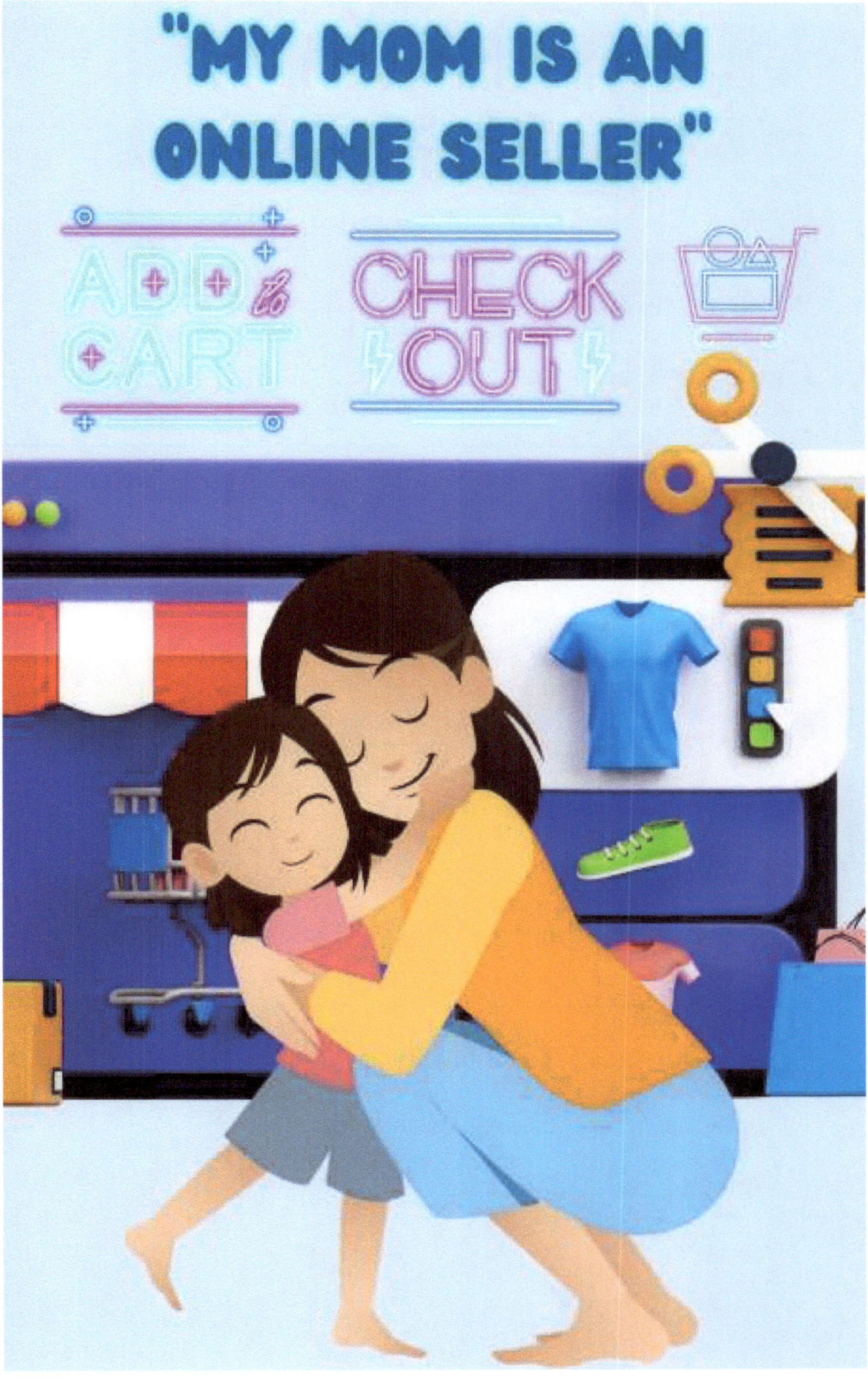
"MY MOM IS AN ONLINE SELLER"
ADD to CART
CHECK OUT

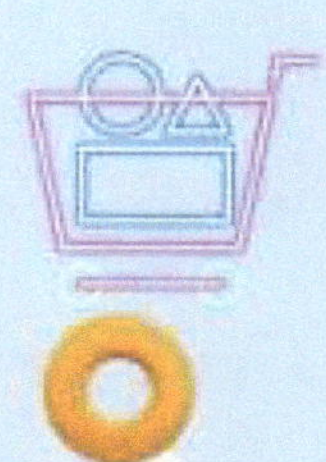

MY MOM IS AN ONLINE SELLER

My Mama Ann is truly a treasure,

As an online seller, she brings pleasure,

Her joy and devotion,

Has made a good inspiration.

She works early every day,

To make certain her stuff is on display,

From foods to frozen, chocolate and toys,

She sells to parents of girls and boys.

Her clients and customers hold dear her work,

They constantly come back with a smirk,

She has earned a name for herself,

With her tough work and enterprise acumen.

She is a vendor with a heart,

Her buyers have never fled apart,

She continually goes the extra mile,

To make certain they forever smile.

My mom Ann, an online vendor,
Is a real hero, a true seller,
She motivates me more each day,
To chase my ambitions and pave my way.

10 Tips To Sustain As An Online Seller

Being an online vendor can seem like a daunting task for a mother. Finding a happy medium between work and family commitments can be challenging. You may be a prosperous internet vendor and a caring mother if you approach things correctly. Here are some suggestions to help you along the way.

1. Separate your job time from your family time by sticking to a strict routine. This way, you can provide the care your kids require while still accomplishing your professional goals.

2. Despite the complexity of selling online, make your processes straightforward. Make sure everything is explained clearly and the steps are simple to follow.

3. Get the kids involved; they may be a great source of advice and assistance. Allow them to chip in and feel like they have a stake in the company.

4. Use positive reinforcement by praising your kids when they help and rewarding them when they do a good job. This will make them feel appreciated, encouraging them to contribute more.

5. You should make plans for each day, but leave room in your schedule for anything that might come up.

6. It's crucial for a mother and company owner to take time off to relax and refocus. In this way, you can maintain your vitality and enthusiasm all day long.

7. Join online organizations or networks of mothers in a similar position to yours to broaden your reach and gain the support of other mothers.

8. Use automated responses and social media scheduling tools to make your workday more efficient; technology is on your side.

9. To make the best use of your time, you need to prioritize your responsibilities.

10. Be kind and patient with yourself; it's normal to make mistakes, so try not to be too hard on yourself. You're giving it your all, and that's the most important thing.

You may be a successful online vendor and a responsible mother by following these guidelines, which include making a timetable, incorporating your children, maintaining some degree of flexibility, networking, and more. As you embark on the adventure of parenthood and enterprise, remember to take breaks and be kind to yourself.

ABOUT THE AUTHORS

ANN COMPIO DOMINGO

A mom, online seller, and loving wife. She is the owner of AJ Delicacies and Stuff with 6 thousand followers. She is altruistic. She loves helping the kids in Catechism class. She dedicate her life to loving her two gems "Mirjana and Avery". Her perseverance, patience, and faith in God have sustained her in online selling.

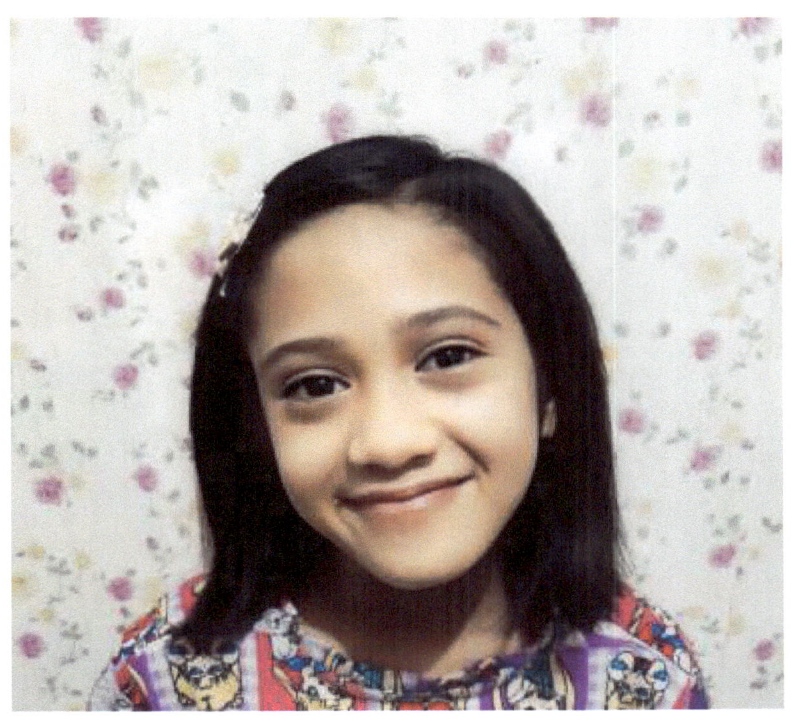

MIRJANA IVANKA COMPIO

Grade 5 Student (incoming grade 6 student) and consistently one of the top students in the class. Member of the Traditional Latin Mass Community in Bacolod. Junior Catechist (Stella Matutina Cherubs). Book Author of Catholic Children's Book “Pinkie Got Her New Eyes" .

BIMBY MACBS COMPIO

Bimby Macbs is a Registered Nurse in the Philippines and has worked as an Academe Marketing and Sales Specialist.

He will be receiving his Doctor in Literature this April of 2023

He decides to discontinue his job and focus on freelance writing, catechism, and evangelization. He is a seminar lecturer, and career coach, conducting career orientation with students in secondary education in preparation for their college program.

He has training in the human temperament, love languages, and psycho-spiritual integration.